LIA'S JOURNEY

by Nancy J. Nielsen
illustrated by William Maughn

MODERN CURRICULUM PRESS

Pearson Learning Group

I sat in the old black truck as it rattled down the road. I slumped as low in the seat as I could next to Gramps, hoping none of my friends would see me.

I was on my way out to the Navajo Reservation for the summer, maybe longer. I'm half Navajo. I'd lived my entire life in Flagstaff, Arizona. But Mom was going away to college in Tucson, and I couldn't go with her.

Mom tried to make the trip sound exciting. "You'll learn all about your heritage," she said.

Mom and I visited the reservation often. Although it was a fun place to visit, I didn't want to live there. My grandparents had no running water and no electricity. I'd miss my friends and my life in Flagstaff.

But staying with Grams and Gramps was my only choice. My father died years ago. Like it or not, Mom's relatives were the only family I had.

Gramps turned off the highway onto a dirt road. We were surrounded by high desert, with nothing but rolling hills for miles. In the distance I could see adobe houses atop the mesas.

4

Gramps turned again, and then stopped in front of an aging hogan, a little dwelling built from lumber and filled in with mud. Behind the hogan was a sheep corral. I heard horses whinny in the barn. Several trucks sat nearby. My cousin Seth watched TV in one of them. The TV was powered by the truck's battery. I could smell stew and fry bread before I even entered the house. That's what they often ate out here.

The house was full of relatives, including my cousin, Birdie. She and her family stayed with Grams, especially when Gramps was away working for the railroad. As I curled under a quilt on the sofa that night, I wondered if I would ever feel at home in this crowded place.

The next morning, I helped Grams take the sheep to the windmill for watering. The windmill pumps water into a large tank where the sheep can drink. Grams used to have more than three hundred sheep, but now she had only five.

We mounted horses and led the sheep onto the grasslands. The grass was long, lush, and green. We took our time as the sheep stopped now and then to graze.

I knew that Grams loved the sheep. She took care of them with such devotion. Her whole life revolved around caring for them and working with their wool.

Grams had planned to leave the sheep and the land to her granddaughters, including me. Mom had told me about my birth in the hogan. According to tradition, I should live the traditional way, and work to turn sheep's wool into rugs and blankets.

Grams was aware of my feelings. She knew it wasn't my choice to live the traditional way with her.

"Give it time, Lia," she said quietly on my first day. "It takes more than a day."

While the sheep drank, Grams poked about the land. Soon she called me over. Using a stick, Grams dug up a strange, rubbery root. She cleaned it off, then popped it into her mouth.

"It's like chewing gum," Grams said, handing me a piece. I remembered the smooth, syrupy root from past visits. While chewing the tasty treat, we rounded up the sheep and herded them back to Grams's place.

"Plop!" I slid a piece of fry bread dough into a pan filled with melted fat. It sizzled as it fried.

"Turn it now," Grams instructed. Then she showed me how to slide the piece out of the pan. I had to admit that Grams's authentic fry bread was delicious!

Grams was intent on teaching me all about my heritage. Learning this heritage kept me busy. We spent time in the garden. We took the sheep to the windmill twice a day for water. Grams gave me my own horse to help with the chore. I loved the honey-colored mare called Sage.

At night, we either cleaned wool or spun it into yarn. We spent one whole week dying wool with berry juice. Then Grams began to teach me how to weave the beautiful traditional rugs and blankets the Navajo are famous for.

Sometimes, Grams and I went to the trading store where Birdie and her mother worked. Grams always brought a rug or a blanket to sell. Then we'd help make the traditional turquoise necklaces.

Birdie showed me how to line up pieces of turquoise on a jewelry board. "Put the largest stones in the middle," she instructed me. "These smaller stones can go on the sides."

Many tourists stopped at the store to buy authentic Navajo rugs, blankets, and jewelry. Because Grams disapproved of a girl wearing jeans, I'd begun to wear the traditional long Navajo skirt. I feared that the tourists saw me as a cute little Navajo girl. I tried to hide behind the counter, but they always found some excuse to talk to me. "Do you speak English?" one woman asked slowly.

"Of course I speak English!" I felt like saying. English was my only language. Although Grams could speak Navajo, my mom had barely learned the language. I had never even been taught Navajo. I wasn't authentic at all, I thought, as I strung another necklace. I still saw myself as just a regular city girl.

One afternoon, Grams sent me alone to the windmill with the sheep. A late August sun blazed across the desert. I slipped my jeans under the long skirt before I left. While the sheep drank, I pulled off the skirt and shoved it in a leather pouch bag.

I wasn't anxious to return to a night of cleaning wool. So I decided I'd take the sheep farther north to the ridge. I filled my water bottle before we went. We set out slowly in the smoldering heat. Ahead lay several large, flat sheets of rock. I decided to rest there and take in some sun. The sheep could continue to graze.

As I slid from the horse to the rock, I thought I heard a rattle. I turned and watched as a snake slithered off the rock into the crevices below. My fingers automatically clutched the pouch around my neck. Grams had given it to me during my first week. It was filled with herbs. "To keep away the rattlesnake," she had said.

Anxiously I glanced around. Should I stay at the rock, I wondered. Was it safe?

The snake was nowhere in sight. Instead I was surrounded by peace and quiet. A slight breeze relaxed me, and I realized I was tired and thirsty, not afraid. Maybe Grams's herbs did work! I sat down to rest.

After a swig of water, I lay back on the rock. The blue sky was interrupted by an occasional white cloud. It was the same sky as the one that was over Flagstaff, I thought. Yet being here seemed so different.

My thoughts drifted with the clouds. I had to admit that summer at Grams's house had not been so bad. I liked eating fry bread with my cousins and making jewelry with Birdie. I loved caring for Sage and taking her out for an afternoon alone. I might even learn to like weaving wool into rugs.

I remembered Grams's words. "It takes more than one day." Maybe what she said was true. Despite my intentions, I had grown to like the rhythms of reservation life.

Three red-tailed hawks circled overhead, disturbing my solitude. Time to leave. My jeans were sweaty. I pulled them off, then slipped on the Navajo skirt. It was cool and full, and would not get in my way as I rode.

Before leaving, I glanced up at the adobe houses on the mesa. The setting sun had turned the adobe village to shadows.

The sheep bleated as I gently rounded them up for home. Whether or not I stayed on the reservation, I had learned about my heritage. I had come to respect the traditional way of life. Perhaps it was more a part of me than I realized. Being Navajo was something I would always value.